Conquering Shame Journal

A Guided Reflection Experience

By
Lakisha Foxworth, LMFT

Conquering
Shame Journal

Lakisha Foxworth, LMFT

© Copyright2023. Updated 2025. by Lakisha Foxworth

Contents

DEDICATION

To God—

Thank You for being my constant source of strength, wisdom, and grace. It is through You that healing flows and purpose is fulfilled. Every word I write is a reflection of Your redemptive power in my life.

To my family—

Your love, patience, and unwavering belief in me have been a cornerstone of my journey. Thank you for encouraging me, even when the path wasn't easy.

To my friends—

Your support, prayers, and reminders to keep going have meant more than you know. Thank you for standing with me, cheering me on, and believing in the vision God placed in my heart.

This journal is for every soul seeking freedom — may you find healing, hope, and the courage to conquer shame.

IDENTIFYING SHAME

Identify things that make you feel shame.

_____

_____

_____

_____

_____

_____

_____

_____

_____

_____

_____

_____

_____

_____

_____

_____

What has shame stopped you from doing? Career? Personal relationships?

_____

_____

_____

_____

_____

_____

_____

_____

_____

_____

_____

_____

_____

_____

_____

_____

_____

_____

_____

_____

What is something shame has caused you to do? Describe the cycle you find yourself in?

_____

_____

_____

_____

_____

_____

_____

_____

_____

_____

_____

_____

_____

_____

_____

_____

_____

_____

SHAME'S IMPACT

In what ways has shame manifested itself in your life? Physically, Mentally? Emotionally? Spiritually?

_____

_____

_____

_____

_____

_____

_____

_____

_____

_____

_____

_____

_____

_____

_____

_____

Is there any proof to support the negative thoughts derived from shame that you have about yourself? Put those thoughts on trial

_____

_____

_____

_____

_____

_____

_____

_____

_____

_____

_____

_____

_____

_____

_____

_____

_____

_____

_____

When you were a child, what happened when you made a mistake or didn't meet someone's expectations? Were you harshly criticized or punished?

_____

_____

_____

_____

_____

_____

_____

_____

_____

_____

_____

_____

_____

_____

_____

_____

_____

_____

HEALING THE INNER CHILD

If you could go back in time, what would you say to your younger self when you felt scared, worried, inadequate, ashamed?

_____

_____

_____

_____

_____

_____

_____

_____

_____

_____

_____

_____

_____

_____

_____

_____

What is holding you back right now? How can you choose to move forward?

SELF-AFFIRMATION

What can you say to remind yourself that you are enough, just as you are?
You may try some positive affirmations.

_____

_____

_____

_____

_____

_____

_____

_____

_____

_____

_____

_____

_____

_____

Which of the following words do you identify with? How does it manifest in your life?

_____

_____

_____

_____

_____

_____

_____

_____

_____

_____

_____

_____

FEAR & REJECTION

Are you fearful of being rejected? What's the root of that fear? Shame? Feelings of being worthless?

_____

_____

_____

_____

_____

_____

_____

_____

_____

_____

_____

_____

_____

_____

_____

_____

_____

Who are you? Really? Take a moment to self-reflect and write about who you are at your core?

_____

_____

_____

_____

_____

_____

_____

_____

_____

_____

_____

_____

_____

_____

_____

_____

_____

_____

_____

_____

_____

RELATIONSHIP & CONNECTION

Shame tends to keep us disconnected. How can you nurture relationships and build connections with others?

_____

_____

_____

_____

_____

_____

_____

_____

_____

_____

_____

_____

_____

_____

_____

_____

GRATITUDE & FORGIVENESS

Many times we focus our attention on the negative aspects of life. It helps to shift our focus on things we can be thankful for. List them below.

_____

_____

_____

_____

_____

_____

_____

_____

_____

_____

_____

_____

_____

_____

_____

GRATITUDE & FORGIVENESS

Forgiveness, who do you need to forgive for not supporting you, hurting you? Others? Self?

_____

_____

_____

_____

_____

_____

_____

_____

_____

_____

_____

_____

_____

_____

_____

_____

_____

_____

STRENGTH & RESILIENCE

What are some challenges you have overcome? How? Lessons learned?

_____

_____

_____

_____

_____

_____

_____

_____

_____

_____

_____

_____

_____

_____

_____

_____

STRENGTH & RESILIENCE

Identify your strengths? Things you are good at?

_____

_____

_____

_____

_____

_____

_____

_____

_____

_____

_____

_____

_____

_____

_____

_____

_____

_____

DREAMS & GOALS

What would you do if you knew you could not fail? What dream would you work to make a reality?

_____

_____

_____

_____

_____

_____

_____

_____

_____

_____

_____

_____

_____

_____

_____

What are 3 things you have done for others that made you feel good on the inside?

_____

_____

_____

_____

_____

_____

_____

_____

_____

_____

_____

_____

_____

_____

_____

_____

_____

_____

What is something you can do today to show yourself love?

_____

_____

_____

_____

_____

_____

_____

_____

_____

_____

_____

_____

_____

_____

_____

_____

_____

_____

POSITIVE EXPERIENCES & REGRET

I had a positive experience with (person, place or thing)? Describe the experience in detail.

_____

_____

_____

_____

_____

_____

_____

_____

_____

_____

_____

_____

_____

_____

_____

What is something you regret not doing? Can you still do it?

SELF-IMAGE & IDENTITY

Describe yourself in five words that come to mind. Then list 5 words that you'd like to describe yourself. List a few ways to make them a reality.

_____

_____

_____

_____

_____

_____

_____

_____

_____

_____

_____

_____

_____

_____

_____

What three things would you most like others (friends, loved ones, professional acquaintances, potential mates) to know about you?

_____

_____

_____

_____

_____

_____

_____

_____

_____

_____

_____

_____

_____

_____

_____

_____

_____

_____

_____

EMOTIONS & COPING

What are three things that can instantly disrupt a good mood and bring you down?

_____

_____

_____

_____

_____

_____

_____

_____

_____

_____

_____

_____

_____

_____

_____

What are your go-to coping strategies that help you get through moments of emotional or physical pain? Are they helpful or harmful?

_____

_____

_____

_____

_____

_____

_____

_____

_____

_____

_____

_____

_____

_____

_____

_____

_____

_____

_____

Which emotions do you find are hardest to accept (anger, shame, guilt, disappointment etc.)? Why? How do you manage them?

_____

_____

_____

_____

_____

_____

_____

_____

_____

_____

_____

_____

_____

_____

_____

_____

_____

_____

JOY & CONTENTMENT

What is something you don't do enough of?

_____

_____

_____

_____

_____

_____

_____

_____

_____

_____

_____

_____

_____

_____

_____

What was something that made you smile today?

_____

_____

_____

_____

_____

_____

_____

_____

_____

_____

_____

_____

_____

_____

_____

_____

_____

_____

What is one thing you would never change about yourself?

_____

_____

_____

_____

_____

_____

_____

_____

_____

_____

_____

_____

_____

_____

_____

_____

_____

_____

_____

Do you make time for yourself each day? If so, how? If not, how can you start to do this?

_____

_____

_____

_____

_____

_____

_____

_____

_____

_____

_____

_____

_____

_____

_____

_____

_____

_____

_____

www.ingramcontent.com/pod-product-compliance
Lightning Source LLC
Chambersburg PA
CBHW080217040426
42331CB00036B/3282